Computerised Accounting Practice Set Using MYOB AccountRight

Advanced Level

This advanced level computerised accounting practice set is for students who need to practice exercises of MYOB AccountRight software, students can record a month's transactions of Richmond Papers Pty Ltd and can create financial reports.

It covers the following topics.

- a) Setting Up a New Accounting System
- b) Integrated Business Transactions
- c) Bank Reconciliation
- d) Financial Reports

Syed Tirmizi
Certified Advisor

ISBN 978-0-9945988-1-3

9 780994 598813 >

For enquiries, please contact **syed.tirmizi@mail.com**

Part A
Practice Set

This page is blank.

Instructions

You have recently been appointed as an Accounts Assistant at Richmond Papers Pty Ltd, a new business dealing in printing and publishing. Your responsibilities are to set up a computerised accounting system, update the company records and produce financial reports.

They started their trading from 1st April 2016. For the first two months the owner of the business, John Smith practiced manual accounting, as the business grew he decided to switch to MYOB AccountRight from 1st June 2016. All documents have been checked for accuracy.

The company uses straight line method for depreciating its non-current assets at 10% yearly. The policy defines the decline in value of these non-current assets on monthly basis.

You are required to complete the following tasks for the month of June 2016 in the order given.

a) Setting Up a New Accounting System
b) Integrated Business Transactions
c) Bank Reconciliation
d) Financial Reports

a) Setting Up a New Accounting System

Create the following data file in MYOB AccountRight Plus for Richmond Papers Pty Ltd.

Company Details	
Company Name	Richmond Papers Pty Ltd
ABN	46 995 263 632
Address	23 High Street, Richmond VIC 3121
Phone Number	03 9876 5432
Financial Year	01-Jul-15 to 30-Jun-16
Conversion Month	June
Accounts List	Start with an accounts list provided by MYOB
Industry	Retail

Enter account opening balances from the Trial Balance given in the Table 1. You may need to add or edit accounts as necessary. Make sure that all header accounts display a subtotal for their group.

Set up Suppliers, Customers and Items together with their opening balances with the help of Tables 2, 3, 4 and 5.

Print or save the following reports for May 2016 before moving to the next section.

i. Trial Balance
ii. Payable Reconciliation (Summary)
iii. Receivables Reconciliation (Summary)
iv. Inventory Value Reconciliation (1st Jun 2016)

Table 1: Opening Balances as at 31st May 2016

Account No.	Account Name	Account Balance
1-1110	Cheque Account	$23,490.88
1-1310	Trade Debtors	$31,250.00
1-1320	Inventory	$8,827.53
1-2110	Furniture At Cost	$8,000.00
1-2120	Accum. Depr. Furniture	-$266.00
1-2210	Office Equipment At Cost	$7,000.00
1-2220	Accum. Depr. Office Equipment	-$234.00
1-2310	Computers At Cost	$5,000.00
1-2320	Accum. Depr. Computers	-$166.00
1-2410	Store Fittings At Cost	$15,000.00
1-2420	Accum. Depr. Store Fittings	-$500.00
2-1210	GST Collected	$7,574.39
2-1220	GST Paid	-$5,931.76
2-1510	Trade Creditors	$22,275.00
2-2100	Bank Loan	$19,631.93
3-1000	Owner's Capital	$30,000.00
4-1000	Sales - A3 Copy Paper	$17,272.73
4-2000	Sales - A4 Copy Paper	$11,863.65
4-3000	Sales - A5 Copy Paper	$18,772.72
4-4000	Sales - Coloured Paper	$10,545.45
4-5000	Sales – Envelopes	$5,886.37
4-6000	Sales - Register Rolls	$11,781.81
5-1000	Cost Of Sales	$47,222.72
6-1700	Electricity Expenses	$370.72
6-2000	Telephone Expenses	$399.64
6-3000	Waste Removal	$100.00
6-3500	Discounts Given	$378.87
6-5100	Furniture Depreciation	$266.00
6-5200	Office Equipment Depreciation	$234.00
6-5300	Computer Depreciation	$166.00
6-5400	Store Fittings Depreciation	$500.00
6-7100	Business Insurance	$400.00
6-8100	Rent	$2,000.00
9-1000	Interest Expense	$231.93

Table 2: Suppliers

Name	A/C No	Address	Layout	Credit Limit
Mark & Tony	MARKA001	41 Middleborough Road, St Albans, VIC 3021	Item	$10,000
Opening Balance	**Terms**	**ABN**	**Tax Code**	**Freight Tax Code**
$4,900 – Purch # 0014	No. of days 30	84 678 592 583	GST	GST

Name	A/C No	Address	Layout	Credit Limit
David & Sons	DAVID001	67 Longwood Road, Craigieburn, VIC 3064	Item	$15,000
Opening Balance	**Terms**	**ABN**	**Tax Code**	**Freight Tax Code**
$0	No. of days 30	65 473 985 624	GST	GST

Name	A/C No	Address	Layout	Credit Limit
Ian & Co. Pty Ltd	IANAN001	94 High Street, Fitzroy, VIC 3065	Item	$6,000
Opening Balance	**Terms**	**ABN**	**Tax Code**	**Freight Tax Code**
$4,000 - Purch # 0013	No. of days 30	25 657 917 634	GST	GST

Name	A/C No	Address	Layout	Credit Limit
Smith & Baker	SMITH001	11 Westfield Road, Lalor, VIC 3075	Item	$10,000
Opening Balance	**Terms**	**ABN**	**Tax Code**	**Freight Tax Code**
$4,000 - Purch # 0012	No. of days 30	54 637 945 746	GST	GST

Name	A/C No	Address	Layout	Credit Limit
Gary Corporation	GARYC001	94 Wellington Street, Preston, VIC 3072	Item	$15,000
Opening Balance	**Terms**	**ABN**	**Tax Code**	**Freight Tax Code**
$9,375 - Purch # 0011	No. of days 30	74 325 496 324	GST	GST

Name	A/C No	Address	Layout	Credit Limit
East End Pty Ltd	EASTE001	34 Canterbury Road, Epping, VIC 3076	Item	$5,000
Opening Balance	**Terms**	**ABN**	**Tax Code**	**Freight Tax Code**
$0	No. of days 30	96 376 843 587	GST	GST

Table 3: Utilities Suppliers

Name	A/C No	Address	Layout	Credit Limit
Victoria Electricity	VICTO001	122 West Street, Melbourne, VIC 3000	Service	$0
Opening Balance	**Terms**	**ABN**	**Tax Code**	**Freight Tax Code**
$0	No. of Days 7	58 687 955 650	GST	GST

Name	A/C No	Address	Layout	Credit Limit
Australia Telecom	AUSTR001	Level 3, 285 Ruth Street, Sydney, NSW 2000	Service	$0
Opening Balance	**Terms**	**ABN**	**Tax Code**	**Freight Tax Code**
$0	No. of Days 7	91 987 654 322	GST	GST

Name	A/C No	Address	Layout	Credit Limit
Richmond Real Estate	RICHM001	233 Richmond Road, Richmond, VIC 3121	Service	$0
Opening Balance	**Terms**	**ABN**	**Tax Code**	**Freight Tax Code**
$0	Prepaid	12 192 837 455	GST	GST

Name	A/C No	Address	Layout	Credit Limit
Melbourne Insurance	MELBO001	100 Lonsdale Street, Fitzroy, VIC 3065	Service	$0
Opening Balance	**Terms**	**ABN**	**Tax Code**	**Freight Tax Code**
$0	Prepaid	76 887 678 654	GST	GST

Name	A/C No	Address	Layout	Credit Limit
Melbourne Removals	MELBO002	55 Mitcham Road, Melbourne, VIC 3000	Service	$0
Opening Balance	**Terms**	**ABN**	**Tax Code**	**Freight Tax Code**
$0	No. of Days 7	67 678 876 764	GST	GST

Table 4: Customers

Name	A/C No	Address	Layout	Credit Limit
Peter Electronics	PETER001	9 Western Avenue, Brooklyn - VIC 3012	Item	$10,000
Opening Balance	**Terms**	**ABN**	**Tax Code**	**Freight Tax Code**
$10,000 - Inv # 0015	No. of days 30	52 639 846 324	GST	GST

Name	A/C No	Address	Layout	Credit Limit
Western Estate Agents	WESTE001	362 High Street, Sunshine - VIC 3020	Item	$10,000
Opening Balance	**Terms**	**ABN**	**Tax Code**	**Freight Tax Code**
$4,500 - Inv # 0016	No. of days 30	47 528 963 764	GST	GST

Name	A/C No	Address	Layout	Credit Limit
Surf Stores	SURFS001	54 Dundee Street, Deer Park, VIC 3023	Item	$10,000
Opening Balance	**Terms**	**ABN**	**Tax Code**	**Freight Tax Code**
$8,400 - Inv # 0017	No. of days 30	95 768 359 862	GST	GST

Name	A/C No	Address	Layout	Credit Limit
Sally's Warehouse	SALLY001	12 Wood Street, Essendon, VIC 3040	Item	$15,000
Opening Balance	**Terms**	**ABN**	**Tax Code**	**Freight Tax Code**
$8,350 - Inv # 0018	No. of days 30	76 662 485 964	GST	GST

Name	A/C No	Address	Layout	Credit Limit
Horizon Designs	HORIZ001	32 Abbots Road, Broadmeadows, VIC 3047	Item	$6,000
Opening Balance	**Terms**	**ABN**	**Tax Code**	**Freight Tax Code**
$0	No. of days 30	12 528 972 562	GST	GST

Name	A/C No	Address	Layout	Credit Limit
Thomson Clothings	THOMS001	84 Spring Street, Thomastown, VIC 3074	Item	$5,000
Opening Balance	**Terms**	**ABN**	**Tax Code**	**Freight Tax Code**
$0	No. of days 30	74 635 842 321	GST	GST

Name	A/C No	Address	Layout	Credit Limit
Globe Travels Pty Ltd	GLOBE001	42 Barry Road, Melbourne, VIC 3000	Item	$10,000
Opening Balance	**Terms**	**ABN**	**Tax Code**	**Freight Tax Code**
$0	No. of days 30	85 365 412 741	GST	GST

Name	A/C No	Address	Layout	Credit Limit
Tiffany Cakes	TIFFA001	36 High Road, Williamstown, VIC 3016	Item	$10,000
Opening Balance	**Terms**	**ABN**	**Tax Code**	**Freight Tax Code**
$0	No. of days 30	78 635 254 524	GST	GST

Table 5: Items List

Profile	Item 1	Item 2	Item 3	Item 4	Item 5	Item 6
Item Number	A3CP	A4CP	A5CP	COLO	EN01	RR18
Name	A3 Copy Paper	A4 Copy Paper	A5 Copy Paper	Coloured Paper	Envelopes Large	Register Rolls
I Buy This Item	✓	✓	✓	✓	✓	✓
I Sell This Item	✓	✓	✓	✓	✓	✓
I Inventory This Item	✓	✓	✓	✓	✓	✓
Cost of Sales Account	5-1000	5-1000	5-1000	5-1000	5-1000	5-1000
Income Account for Tracking Sales	4-1000	4-2000	4-3000	4-4000	4-5000	4-6000
Asset Account for Item Inventory	1-1320	1-1320	1-1320	1-1320	1-1320	1-1320
Buying Details						
Buying Unit of Measure	each	each	each	each	box	box
Number of Items per Buying Unit	1	1	1	1	1	1
Tax Code When Bought	GST	GST	GST	GST	GST	GST
Selling Details						
Base Selling Price ($)	40	15	14	20	35	54
Selling Unit of Measure	each	each	each	each	box	box
Number of Items per Selling Unit	1	1	1	1	1	1
Tax Code When Sold	GST	GST	GST	GST	GST	GST
Prices are Tax Inclusive	✓	✓	✓	✓	✓	✓
Calculate Sales Tax on	Actual selling price	Actual selling price	Actual selling price	Actual selling price	Actual selling price	Actual selling price
Balance as at May 31st 2016	250	230	5	70	10	10
Unit Cost Excluding GST	$22.73	$7.27	$7.27	$12.73	$20.00	$34.55

b) Integrated Business Transactions

The following transactions occurred during the month of June 2016.

1st Jun   Paid June rent in advance to Richmond Real Estate by Cheque # 28. Amount $1100.00 including GST.

2nd Jun   Goods purchased.

Supplier	Purchase #	Supplier Inv #	Qty	Item #	Item Name	Price
Gary Corporation	0015	412	40	A3CP	A3 Copy Paper	$25.00
Smith & Baker	0016	G/749	250	A5CP	A5 Copy Paper	$8.00

3rd Jun   Electronic Payment received in Cheque Account from Peter Electronics, Amount $10,000 and Ref # CR0011.

4th Jun   Purchase returned.

Supplier	Purchase #	Supplier Inv #	Qty	Item #	Item Name	Price
Smith & Baker	0017	G/749	20	A5CP	A5 Copy Paper	$8.00

4th Jun   Goods purchased.

Supplier	Purchase #	Supplier Inv #	Qty	Item #	Item Name	Price
David & Sons	0018	2016-16	350	RR18	Register Rolls	$38.00

6th Jun   Goods sold.

Customer	Invoice #	Qty	Item #	Item Name	Price
Horizon Designs	0019	70	A4CP	A4 Copy Paper	$14.50
		60	RR18	Register Rolls	$54.00
		70	A5CP	A5 Copy Paper	$14.00

6th Jun   Goods purchased.

Supplier	Purchase #	Supplier Inv #	Qty	Item #	Item Name	Price
Ian & Co. Pty Ltd	0019	00854	250	A4CP	A4 Copy Paper	$8.00

6th Jun   Electronic Payment received in Cheque Account from Surf Stores, Amount $8,400, Ref # CR0012.

7th Jun   Goods purchased.

Supplier	Purchase #	Supplier Inv #	Qty	Item #	Item Name	Price
Mark & Tony	0020	A423	200	COLO	Coloured Paper	$14.00

7th Jun   Paid Insurance to Melbourne Insurance by Cheque # 29, Amount $220.00 Including GST.

9th Jun   Paid to Gary Corporation by Cheque # 30, Amount $9,375 for the Invoice # 0011.

9th Jun — Goods purchased.

9th Jun   Goods purchased.

Supplier	Purchase #	Supplier Inv #	Qty	Item #	Item Name	Price
East End Pty Ltd	0021	EE2141	200	EN01	Envelopes	$22.00

10th Jun   Goods sold.

Customer	Invoice #	Qty	Item #	Item Name	Price
Thomson Clothings	0020	60	A4CP	A4 Copy Paper	$15.00
		80	EN01	Envelopes Large	$35.00

10th Jun   Electronic Payment received in Cheque Account from Sally's Warehouse, Amount $8,350 and Ref CR0013.

11th Jun   Purchase returned.

Supplier	Purchase #	Supplier Inv #	Qty	Item #	Item Name	Price
David & Sons	0022	2016-16	25	RR18	Register Rolls	$38.00

13th Jun   Electronic Payment received in Cheque Account from Western Estate Agents, Amount $4,500 and Ref CR0014.

13th Jun   Goods sold.

Customer	Invoice #	Qty	Item #	Item Name	Price
Globe Travels Pty Ltd	0021	60	A4CP	A4 Copy Paper	$15.00
		50	A3CP	A3 Copy Paper	$40.00
		70	RR18	Register Rolls	$54.00
		60	COLO	Coloured Paper	$20.00

13th Jun   Electronic Payment received in Cheque Account from Horizon Designs, Amount $5,235 and Ref CR0015.

14th Jun   Goods sold.

Customer	Invoice #	Qty	Item #	Item Name	Price
Tiffany Cakes	0022	50	A4CP	A4 Copy Paper	$15.00
		60	RR18	Register Rolls	$54.00
		60	EN01	Envelopes Large	$35.00

16th Jun   Paid to Smith & Baker by Cheque # 31, Amount $4,000 for the Invoice # 0012.

17th Jun   Sales returned.

Customer	Invoice #	Qty	Item #	Item Name	Price
Thomson Clothings	0023	20	EN01	Envelopes Large	$35.00

18th Jun   Electronic Payment received in Cheque Account from Thomson Clothings, Amount $3,000 and Ref CR0016.

18th Jun   Goods sold.

Customer	Invoice #	Qty	Item #	Item Name	Price
Peter Electronics	0024	60	A4CP	A4 Copy Paper	$15.00
		70	COLO	Coloured Paper	$20.00

20th Jun   Paid Electricity Bill to Victoria Electricity by Cheque # 32, Amount $194.40 including GST.

20th Jun   Electronic Payment received in Cheque Account from Globe Travels Pty Ltd, Amount $7,880 and Ref CR0017.

21st Jun   Goods sold.

Customer	Invoice #	Qty	Item #	Item Name	Price
Sally's Warehouse	0025	70	A4CP	A4 Copy Paper	$15.00
		60	COLO	Coloured Paper	$20.00
		70	A3CP	A3 Copy Paper	$40.00
		50	RR18	Register Rolls	$54.00

21st Jun   Paid Telephone Bill to Australia Telecom by Cheque # 33, Amount $215.84 Including GST.

23rd Jun   Sales returned.

Customer	Invoice #	Qty	Item #	Item Name	Price
Sally's Warehouse	0026	10	A4CP	A4 Copy Paper	$15.00

24th Jun   Paid to Ian & Co. Pty Ltd by Cheque # 34, Amount $4,000 for the Invoice # 0013.

25th Jun   Electronic Payment received in Cheque Account from Tiffany Cakes, Amount $6,090 and Ref # CR0018.

25th Jun   Goods sold.

Customer	Invoice #	Qty	Item #	Item Name	Price
Western Estate Agents	0027	100	A5CP	A5 Copy Paper	$14.00

25th Jun   Paid rubbish removal charges to Melbourne Removals by Cheque # 35, Amount $55.00 including GST.

27th Jun   Electronic Payment received in Cheque Account from Peter Electronics, Amount $2,300 and Ref # CR0019.

27th Jun   Goods sold.

Customer	Invoice #	Qty	Item #	Item Name	Price
Surf Stores	0028	50	A4CP	A4 Copy Paper	$15.00
		30	RR18	Register Rolls	$54.00

28th Jun   Paid to Mark & Tony by Cheque # 36, Amount $4,900 for the Purchase # 0014.
                     Paid to Gary Corporation by Cheque # 37, Amount $1,000 for the Purchase # 0015.
                     Paid to Smith & Baker by Cheque # 38, Amount $1,840 for the Purchase # 0016.

30th Jun   Process depreciation on the following assets. Expense and Accumulated Depreciation accounts need to be adjusted by Journal Entry.

Furniture	$133
Office Equipment	$117
Computer	$83
Store Fittings	$250

c) Bank Reconciliation

30th Jun   Prepare bank reconciliation for the month of June 2016. Company bank statement is on the next page.

Following information obtained from loan account regarding the breakdown of $300 direct debit on 30/06/2016. Interest Expense, Bank Loan and Cheque Account need to be adjusted by Journal Entry.

Interest paid	$114.36
Principal amount paid	$185.64

Money taken from the cheque account	$300.00
	======

BANK OF RICHMOND

36 Spring Street, Richmond, VIC 3121
TEL 1800 AUSTRALIA

Cheque Account Statement
30/06/2016

Richmond Papers Pty Ltd
23 High Street
Richmond
VIC 3121

BSB Number	Account Number
654 321	123456789

Date	Details	Ref	Withdrawals	Deposits	Balance
01-Jun-16	Balance brought forward				$23,490.88
03-Jun-16	Transfer – Peter Electronics			$10,000.00	$33,490.88
04-Jun-16	CHQ 00028		$1,100.00		$32,390.88
06-Jun-16	Transfer – Surf Stores			$8,400.00	$40,790.88
09-Jun-16	CHQ 00029		$220.00		$40,570.88
10-Jun-16	Transfer – Sally's Warehouse			$8,350.00	$48,920.88
11-Jun-16	CHQ 00030		$9,375.00		$39,545.88
13-Jun-16	Transfer – Western Estate Agents			$4,500.00	
13-Jun-16	Transfer – Horizon Designs			$5,235.00	$49,280.88
18-Jun-16	Transfer – Thomson Clothings			$3,000.00	$52,280.88
19-Jun-16	CHQ 00031		$4,000.00		$48,280.88
21-Jun-16	CHQ 00032		$194.40		$48,086.48
20-Jun-16	Transfer – Globe Travels Pty Ltd			$7,880.00	$55,966.48
24-Jun-16	CHQ 00033		$215.84		$55,750.64
25-Jun-16	CHQ 00034		$4,000.00		$51,750.64
25-Jun-16	Transfer – Tiffany Cakes			$6,090.00	$57,840.64
27-Jun-16	Transfer – Peter Electronics			$2,300.00	$60,140.64
30-Jun-16	Direct Debit – Loan Account		$300.00		
30-Jun-16	Bank Charges		$18.00		$59,822.64
	Totals		**$19,423.24**	**$55,755.00**	

d) Financial Reports

Print or save the following reports for the month of June 2016.

v.	Bank Register for account 1-1110
vi.	Purchases & Payables Journal
vii.	Cash Disbursements Journal
viii.	Sales & Receivables Journal
ix.	Cash Receipts Journal
x.	Items Register Detail
xi.	General Journal
xii.	Bank Reconciliation Report
xiii.	Profit & Loss Statement
xiv.	Trial Balance
xv.	Balance Sheet

Part B
Solutions

Trial Balance

May 2016

Richmond Papars Pty Ltd
23 High Street
Richmond
VIC 3121

ABN: 46 995 263 632

Account Name	Debit	Credit	YTD Debit	YTD Credit
Cheque Account	$23,490.88		$23,490.88	
Trade Debtors	$31,250.00		$31,250.00	
Inventory	$8,827.53		$8,827.53	
Furniture At Cost	$8,000.00		$8,000.00	
Accum. Depr. Furniture		$266.00		$266.00
Office Equipment At Cost	$7,000.00		$7,000.00	
Accum. Depr. Office Equipment		$234.00		$234.00
Computers At Cost	$5,000.00		$5,000.00	
Accum. Depr. Computers		$166.00		$166.00
Store Fittings At Cost	$15,000.00		$15,000.00	
Accum. Depr. Store Fittings		$500.00		$500.00
GST Collected		$7,574.39		$7,574.39
GST Paid	$5,931.76		$5,931.76	
Trade Creditors		$22,275.00		$22,275.00
Bank Loan		$19,631.93		$19,631.93
Owner's Capital		$30,000.00		$30,000.00
Sales - A3 Copy Paper		$17,272.73		$17,272.73
Sales - A4 Copy Paper		$11,863.65		$11,863.65
Sales - A5 Copy Paper		$18,772.72		$18,772.72
Sales - Coloured Paper		$10,545.45		$10,545.45
Sales - Envelopes		$5,886.37		$5,886.37
Sales - Register Rolls		$11,781.81		$11,781.81
Cost Of Sales	$47,222.72		$47,222.72	
Electricity Expenses	$370.72		$370.72	
Telephone Expenses	$399.64		$399.64	
Waste Removal	$100.00		$100.00	
Discounts Given	$378.87		$378.87	
Furniture Depreciation	$266.00		$266.00	
Office Equipment Depreciation	$234.00		$234.00	
Computer Depreciation	$166.00		$166.00	
Store Fittings Depreciation	$500.00		$500.00	
Business Insurance	$400.00		$400.00	
Rent	$2,000.00		$2,000.00	
Interest Expense	$231.93		$231.93	
Total:	$156,770.05	$156,770.05	$156,770.05	$156,770.05

This report includes Year-End Adjustments.

Richmond Papars Pty Ltd
23 High Street
Richmond
VIC 3121

Payables Reconciliation [Summary]

As of 31-May-16

ABN: 46 995 263 632

Name	Total Due	0 - 30	31 - 60	61 - 90	90+
Gary Corporation	$9,375.00	$9,375.00	$0.00	$0.00	$0.00
Ian & Co. Pty Ltd	$4,000.00	$4,000.00	$0.00	$0.00	$0.00
Mark & Tony	$4,900.00	$4,900.00	$0.00	$0.00	$0.00
Smith & Baker	$4,000.00	$4,000.00	$0.00	$0.00	$0.00
Total:	$22,275.00	$22,275.00	$0.00	$0.00	$0.00
Ageing Percent:		100.0%	0.0%	0.0%	0.0%
Payables Account:	$22,275.00				
Out of Balance Amount	$0.00				

Page 1 of 1

Richmond Papars Pty Ltd
23 High Street
Richmond
VIC 3121

Receivables Reconciliation [Summary]

As of 31-May-16   ABN: 46 995 263 632

Name	Total Due	0 - 30	31 - 60	61 - 90	90+
Peter Electronics	$10,000.00	$10,000.00	$0.00	$0.00	$0.00
Sally's Warehouse	$8,350.00	$8,350.00	$0.00	$0.00	$0.00
Surf Stores	$8,400.00	$8,400.00	$0.00	$0.00	$0.00
Western Estate Agents	$4,500.00	$4,500.00	$0.00	$0.00	$0.00
Total:	$31,250.00	$31,250.00	$0.00	$0.00	$0.00
Ageing Percent:		100.0%	0.0%	0.0%	0.0%
Receivables Account:	$31,250.00				
Out of Balance Amount	$0.00				

Richmond Papars Pty Ltd
23 High Street
Richmond
VIC 3121

ABN: 46 995 263 632

Inventory Value Reconciliation

As of 01-Jun-16

Item No.	Item Name	On Hand	Current Value
1-1320	**Inventory**		
A3CP	A3 Copy Paper	250	$5,682.50
A4CP	A4 Copy Paper	230	$1,672.10
A5CP	A5 Copy Paper	5	$36.34
COLO	Coloured Paper	70	$891.09
EN01	Envelopes Large	10	$200.00
RR18	Register Rolls	10	$345.49
	Inventory Value:		$8,827.53
	Account Balance:		$8,827.53
	Out of Balance:		$0.00

Page 1 of 1

Richmond Papars Pty Ltd
23 High Street
Richmond
VIC 3121

Bank Register

June 2016

ABN: 46 995 263 632

	ID No.	Src	Date	Memo/Payee	Deposit	Withdrawal	Balance
1-1110		**Cheque Account**					
	28	CD	01-Jun-16	Richmond Real Estate		$1,100.00	$22,390.88
	CR0011	CR	03-Jun-16	Payment; Peter Electronic	$10,000.00		$32,390.88
	CR0012	CR	06-Jun-16	Payment; Surf Stores	$8,400.00		$40,790.88
	29	CD	07-Jun-16	Melbourne Insurance		$220.00	$40,570.88
	30	CD	09-Jun-16	Gary Corporation		$9,375.00	$31,195.88
	CR0013	CR	10-Jun-16	Payment; Sally's Warehou	$8,350.00		$39,545.88
	CR0014	CR	13-Jun-16	Payment; Western Estate	$4,500.00		$44,045.88
	CR0015	CR	13-Jun-16	Payment; Horizon Design	$5,235.00		$49,280.88
	31	CD	16-Jun-16	Smith & Baker		$4,000.00	$45,280.88
	CR0016	CR	18-Jun-16	Payment; Thomson Cloth	$3,000.00		$48,280.88
	32	CD	20-Jun-16	Victoria Electricity		$194.40	$48,086.48
	CR0017	CR	20-Jun-16	Payment; Globe Travels P	$7,880.00		$55,966.48
	33	CD	21-Jun-16	Australia Telecom		$215.84	$55,750.64
	34	CD	24-Jun-16	Ian & Co. Pty Ltd		$4,000.00	$51,750.64
	35	CD	25-Jun-16	Melbourne Removals		$55.00	$51,695.64
	CR0018	CR	25-Jun-16	Payment; Tiffany Cakes	$6,090.00		$57,785.64
	CR0019	CR	27-Jun-16	Payment; Peter Electronic	$2,300.00		$60,085.64
	36	CD	28-Jun-16	Mark & Tony		$4,900.00	$55,185.64
	37	CD	28-Jun-16	Gary Corporation		$1,000.00	$54,185.64
	38	CD	28-Jun-16	Smith & Baker		$1,840.00	$52,345.64
	SC300616	CD	30-Jun-16	Bank Charges		$18.00	$52,327.64
	GJ000002	GJ	30-Jun-16	Loan Instalment Breakdo		$300.00	$52,027.64
					$55,755.00	$27,218.24	

* Year-End Adjustments
Page 1 of 1

Purchases & Payables Journal

Richmond Papars Pty Ltd
23 High Street
Richmond
VIC 3121

01-Jun-16 To 30-Jun-16

ABN: 46 995 263 632

ID No.	Account No.	Account Name	Debit	Credit	Job No.
PJ 02-Jun-16		**Purchase; Gary Corporation**			
00000015	2-1510	Trade Creditors		$1,000.00	
00000015	1-1320	Inventory	$909.09		
00000015	2-1220	GST Paid	$90.91		
PJ 02-Jun-16		**Purchase; Smith & Baker**			
00000016	2-1510	Trade Creditors		$2,000.00	
00000016	1-1320	Inventory	$1,818.18		
00000016	2-1220	GST Paid	$181.82		
PJ 04-Jun-16		**Purchase; Smith & Baker**			
00000017	2-1510	Trade Creditors	$160.00		
00000017	1-1320	Inventory		$145.45	
00000017	2-1220	GST Paid		$14.55	
PJ 04-Jun-16		**Purchase; David & Sons**			
00000018	2-1510	Trade Creditors		$13,300.00	
00000018	1-1320	Inventory	$12,090.91		
00000018	2-1220	GST Paid	$1,209.09		
PJ 04-Jun-16		**Smith & Baker: Debit from 00000017**			
PJ000001	2-1510	Trade Creditors		$160.00	
PJ000001	2-1510	Trade Creditors	$160.00		
PJ 06-Jun-16		**Purchase; Ian & Co. Pty Ltd**			
00000019	2-1510	Trade Creditors		$2,000.00	
00000019	1-1320	Inventory	$1,818.18		
00000019	2-1220	GST Paid	$181.82		
PJ 07-Jun-16		**Purchase; Mark & Tony**			
00000020	2-1510	Trade Creditors		$2,800.00	
00000020	1-1320	Inventory	$2,545.45		
00000020	2-1220	GST Paid	$254.55		
PJ 09-Jun-16		**Purchase; East End Pty Ltd**			
00000021	2-1510	Trade Creditors		$4,400.00	
00000021	1-1320	Inventory	$4,000.00		
00000021	2-1220	GST Paid	$400.00		
PJ 11-Jun-16		**Purchase; David & Sons**			
00000022	2-1510	Trade Creditors	$950.00		
00000022	1-1320	Inventory		$863.64	
00000022	2-1220	GST Paid		$86.36	
PJ 13-Jun-16		**David & Sons: Debit from 00000022**			
PJ000002	2-1510	Trade Creditors		$950.00	
PJ000002	2-1510	Trade Creditors	$950.00		
		Grand Total:	$27,720.00	$27,720.00	

* Year-End Adjustments
Page 1 of 1

Richmond Papars Pty Ltd
23 High Street
Richmond
VIC 3121

Cash Disbursements Journal

01-Jun-16 To 30-Jun-16

ABN: 46 995 263 632

ID No.		Account No.	Account Name	Debit	Credit	Job No.
CD	**01-Jun-16**		Richmond Real Estate 233 Richmond Road Richmond VIC 3121			
28		1-1110	Cheque Account		$1,100.00	
28		6-8100	Rent	$1,000.00		
28		2-1220	GST Paid	$100.00		
CD	**07-Jun-16**		Melbourne Insurance 100 Lonsdale Street Fitzroy VIC 3065			
29		1-1110	Cheque Account		$220.00	
29		6-7100	Business Insurance	$200.00		
29		2-1220	GST Paid	$20.00		
CD	**09-Jun-16**		Gary Corporation 94 Wellington Street Preston VIC 3072			
30		1-1110	Cheque Account		$9,375.00	
30		2-1510	Trade Creditors	$9,375.00		
CD	**16-Jun-16**		Smith & Baker 11 Westfield Road Lalor VIC 3075			
31		1-1110	Cheque Account		$4,000.00	
31		2-1510	Trade Creditors	$4,000.00		
CD	**20-Jun-16**		Victoria Electricity 122 West Street Melbourne VIC 3000			
32		1-1110	Cheque Account		$194.40	
32		6-1700	Electricity Expenses	$176.73		
32		2-1220	GST Paid	$17.67		
CD	**21-Jun-16**		Australia Telecom Level 3, 285 Ruth Street Sydney NSW 2000			
33		1-1110	Cheque Account		$215.84	
33		6-2000	Telephone Expenses	$196.22		
33		2-1220	GST Paid	$19.62		
CD	**24-Jun-16**		Ian & Co. Pty Ltd 94 High Street Fitzroy VIC 3065			
34		1-1110	Cheque Account		$4,000.00	
34		2-1510	Trade Creditors	$4,000.00		
CD	**25-Jun-16**		Melbourne Removals 55 Mitcham Road Melbourne VIC 3000			
35		1-1110	Cheque Account		$55.00	
35		6-3000	Waste Removal	$50.00		
35		2-1220	GST Paid	$5.00		
CD	**28-Jun-16**		Mark & Tony 41 Middleborough Road St. Albans VIC 3021			
36		1-1110	Cheque Account		$4,900.00	
36		2-1510	Trade Creditors	$4,900.00		
CD	**28-Jun-16**		Gary Corporation 94 Wellington Street Preston VIC 3072			
37		1-1110	Cheque Account		$1,000.00	
37		2-1510	Trade Creditors	$1,000.00		
CD	**28-Jun-16**		Smith & Baker 11 Westfield Road Lalor VIC 3075			
38		1-1110	Cheque Account		$1,840.00	
38		2-1510	Trade Creditors	$1,840.00		
CD	**30-Jun-16**		Bank Charges			
SC300616		1-1110	Cheque Account		$18.00	
SC300616		6-1300	Bank Fees	$18.00		
			Grand Total:	$26,918.24	$26,918.24	

* Year-End Adjustments
Page 1 of 1

Richmond Papars Pty Ltd
23 High Street
Richmond
VIC 3121

Sales & Receivables Journal

01-Jun-16 To 30-Jun-16

ABN: 46 995 263 632

ID No.	Account No.	Account Name	Debit	Credit Job No.
SJ 06-Jun-16		**Sale; Horizon Designs**		
00000019	1-1310	Trade Debtors	$5,235.00	
00000019	4-2000	Sales - A4 Copy Paper		$922.73
00000019	4-6000	Sales - Register Rolls		$2,945.45
00000019	4-3000	Sales - A5 Copy Paper		$890.91
00000019	2-1210	GST Collected		$475.91
00000019	1-1320	Inventory		$3,090.73
00000019	5-1000	Cost Of Sales	$3,090.73	
SJ 10-Jun-16		**Sale; Thomson Clothings**		
00000020	1-1310	Trade Debtors	$3,700.00	
00000020	4-2000	Sales - A4 Copy Paper		$818.18
00000020	4-5000	Sales - Envelopes		$2,545.46
00000020	2-1210	GST Collected		$336.36
00000020	1-1320	Inventory		$2,036.30
00000020	5-1000	Cost Of Sales	$2,036.30	
SJ 13-Jun-16		**Sale; Globe Travels Pty Ltd**		
00000021	1-1310	Trade Debtors	$7,880.00	
00000021	4-2000	Sales - A4 Copy Paper		$818.18
00000021	4-1000	Sales - A3 Copy Paper		$1,818.18
00000021	4-6000	Sales - Register Rolls		$3,436.37
00000021	4-4000	Sales - Coloured Paper		$1,090.91
00000021	2-1210	GST Collected		$716.36
00000021	1-1320	Inventory		$4,754.65
00000021	5-1000	Cost Of Sales	$4,754.65	
SJ 14-Jun-16		**Sale; Tiffany Cakes**		
00000022	1-1310	Trade Debtors	$6,090.00	
00000022	4-2000	Sales - A4 Copy Paper		$681.82
00000022	4-6000	Sales - Register Rolls		$2,945.45
00000022	4-5000	Sales - Envelopes		$1,909.09
00000022	2-1210	GST Collected		$553.64
00000022	1-1320	Inventory		$3,636.32
00000022	5-1000	Cost Of Sales	$3,636.32	
SJ 17-Jun-16		**Sale; Thomson Clothings**		
00000023	1-1310	Trade Debtors		$700.00
00000023	4-5000	Sales - Envelopes	$636.36	
00000023	2-1210	GST Collected	$63.64	
00000023	1-1320	Inventory	$400.00	
00000023	5-1000	Cost Of Sales		$400.00
SJ 17-Jun-16		**Thomson Clothings: Credit from 00000023**		
SJ000001	1-1310	Trade Debtors	$700.00	
SJ000001	1-1310	Trade Debtors		$700.00
SJ 18-Jun-16		**Sale; Peter Electronics**		
00000024	1-1310	Trade Debtors	$2,300.00	
00000024	4-2000	Sales - A4 Copy Paper		$818.18
00000024	4-4000	Sales - Coloured Paper		$1,272.73
00000024	2-1210	GST Collected		$209.09
00000024	1-1320	Inventory		$1,327.26
00000024	5-1000	Cost Of Sales	$1,327.26	
SJ 21-Jun-16		**Sale; Sally's Warehouse**		
00000025	1-1310	Trade Debtors	$7,750.00	
00000025	4-2000	Sales - A4 Copy Paper		$954.55
00000025	4-4000	Sales - Coloured Paper		$1,090.90

* Year-End Adjustments
Page 1 of 2

Richmond Papars Pty Ltd
23 High Street
Richmond
VIC 3121

ABN: 46 995 263 632

Sales & Receivables Journal

01-Jun-16 To 30-Jun-16

ID No.	Account No.	Account Name	Debit	Credit	Job No.
00000025	4-1000	Sales - A3 Copy Paper		$2,545.46	
00000025	4-6000	Sales - Register Rolls		$2,454.54	
00000025	2-1210	GST Collected		$704.55	
00000025	1-1320	Inventory		$4,591.04	
00000025	5-1000	Cost Of Sales	$4,591.04		
SJ	**23-Jun-16**	**Sale; Sally's Warehouse**			
00000026	1-1310	Trade Debtors		$150.00	
00000026	4-2000	Sales - A4 Copy Paper	$136.36		
00000026	2-1210	GST Collected	$13.64		
00000026	1-1320	Inventory	$72.72		
00000026	5-1000	Cost Of Sales		$72.72	
SJ	**23-Jun-16**	**Sally's Warehouse: Credit from 00000026**			
SJ000002	1-1310	Trade Debtors	$150.00		
SJ000002	1-1310	Trade Debtors		$150.00	
SJ	**25-Jun-16**	**Sale; Western Estate Agents**			
00000027	1-1310	Trade Debtors	$1,400.00		
00000027	4-3000	Sales - A5 Copy Paper		$1,272.73	
00000027	2-1210	GST Collected		$127.27	
00000027	1-1320	Inventory		$727.27	
00000027	5-1000	Cost Of Sales	$727.27		
SJ	**27-Jun-16**	**Sale; Surf Stores**			
00000028	1-1310	Trade Debtors	$2,370.00		
00000028	4-2000	Sales - A4 Copy Paper		$681.82	
00000028	4-6000	Sales - Register Rolls		$1,472.73	
00000028	2-1210	GST Collected		$215.45	
00000028	1-1320	Inventory		$1,399.95	
00000028	5-1000	Cost Of Sales	$1,399.95		
		Grand Total:	$60,461.24	$60,461.24	

* Year-End Adjustments
Page 2 of 2

Created: 10-May-16 6:35 PM

Richmond Papars Pty Ltd
23 High Street
Richmond
VIC 3121

Cash Receipts Journal

ABN: 46 995 263 632

01-Jun-16 To 30-Jun-16

ID No.	Account No.	Account Name	Debit	Credit	Job No.
CR 03-Jun-16		**Payment; Peter Electronics**			
CR0011	1-1110	Cheque Account	$10,000.00		
CR0011	1-1310	Trade Debtors		$10,000.00	
CR 06-Jun-16		**Payment; Surf Stores**			
CR0012	1-1110	Cheque Account	$8,400.00		
CR0012	1-1310	Trade Debtors		$8,400.00	
CR 10-Jun-16		**Payment; Sally's Warehouse**			
CR0013	1-1110	Cheque Account	$8,350.00		
CR0013	1-1310	Trade Debtors		$8,350.00	
CR 13-Jun-16		**Payment; Western Estate Agents**			
CR0014	1-1110	Cheque Account	$4,500.00		
CR0014	1-1310	Trade Debtors		$4,500.00	
CR 13-Jun-16		**Payment; Horizon Designs**			
CR0015	1-1110	Cheque Account	$5,235.00		
CR0015	1-1310	Trade Debtors		$5,235.00	
CR 18-Jun-16		**Payment; Thomson Clothings**			
CR0016	1-1110	Cheque Account	$3,000.00		
CR0016	1-1310	Trade Debtors		$3,000.00	
CR 20-Jun-16		**Payment; Globe Travels Pty Ltd**			
CR0017	1-1110	Cheque Account	$7,880.00		
CR0017	1-1310	Trade Debtors		$7,880.00	
CR 25-Jun-16		**Payment; Tiffany Cakes**			
CR0018	1-1110	Cheque Account	$6,090.00		
CR0018	1-1310	Trade Debtors		$6,090.00	
CR 27-Jun-16		**Payment; Peter Electronics**			
CR0019	1-1110	Cheque Account	$2,300.00		
CR0019	1-1310	Trade Debtors		$2,300.00	
		Grand Total:	$55,755.00	$55,755.00	

* Year-End Adjustments
Page 1 of 1

Richmond Papars Pty Ltd
23 High Street
Richmond
VIC 3121

Items Register [Detail]

01-Jun-16 To 30-Jun-16

ABN: 46 995 263 632

Date	Src	ID No.	Memo	Starting Qty	Qty Changed	Amount	On Hand	Current Value
A3CP			**A3 Copy Paper**					
01-Jun-16	IJ	IJ000001	Inventory coun	0	250	$5,682.50	250	$5,682.50
02-Jun-16	PJ	00000015	Purchase; Gary	250	40	$909.09	290	$6,591.59
13-Jun-16	SJ	00000021	Sale; Globe Tra	290	-50	($1,136.48)	240	$5,455.11
21-Jun-16	SJ	00000025	Sale; Sally's Wa	240	-70	($1,591.07)	170	$3,864.04
			A3 Copy Pape		170	$3,864.04		
A4CP			**A4 Copy Paper**					
01-Jun-16	IJ	IJ000001	Inventory coun	0	230	$1,672.10	230	$1,672.10
06-Jun-16	SJ	00000019	Sale; Horizon C	230	-70	($508.90)	160	$1,163.20
06-Jun-16	PJ	00000019	Purchase; Ian 8	160	250	$1,818.18	410	$2,981.38
10-Jun-16	SJ	00000020	Sale; Thomson	410	-60	($436.30)	350	$2,545.08
13-Jun-16	SJ	00000021	Sale; Globe Tra	350	-60	($436.30)	290	$2,108.78
14-Jun-16	SJ	00000022	Sale; Tiffany Ca	290	-50	($363.58)	240	$1,745.20
18-Jun-16	SJ	00000024	Sale; Peter Elec	240	-60	($436.30)	180	$1,308.90
21-Jun-16	SJ	00000025	Sale; Sally's Wa	180	-70	($509.01)	110	$799.89
23-Jun-16	SJ	00000026	Sale; Sally's Wa	110	10	$72.72	120	$872.60
27-Jun-16	SJ	00000028	Sale; Surf Store	120	-50	($363.58)	70	$509.02
			A4 Copy Pape		70	$509.02		
A5CP			**A5 Copy Paper**					
01-Jun-16	IJ	IJ000001	Inventory coun	0	5	$36.35	5	$36.34
02-Jun-16	PJ	00000016	Purchase; Smitl	5	250	$1,818.18	255	$1,854.52
04-Jun-16	PJ	00000017	Purchase; Smitl	255	-20	($145.45)	235	$1,709.07
06-Jun-16	SJ	00000019	Sale; Horizon C	235	-70	($509.09)	165	$1,199.99
25-Jun-16	SJ	00000027	Sale; Western E	165	-100	($727.27)	65	$472.72
			A5 Copy Pape		65	$472.73		
COLO			**Coloured Paper**					
01-Jun-16	IJ	IJ000001	Inventory coun	0	70	$891.10	70	$891.09
07-Jun-16	PJ	00000020	Purchase; Mark	70	200	$2,545.45	270	$3,436.54
13-Jun-16	SJ	00000021	Sale; Globe Tra	270	-60	($763.68)	210	$2,672.86
18-Jun-16	SJ	00000024	Sale; Peter Elec	210	-70	($890.96)	140	$1,781.91
21-Jun-16	SJ	00000025	Sale; Sally's Wa	140	-60	($763.68)	80	$1,018.23
			Coloured Pape		80	$1,018.24		
EN01			**Envelopes Large**					
01-Jun-16	IJ	IJ000001	Inventory coun	0	10	$200.00	10	$200.00
09-Jun-16	PJ	00000021	Purchase; East	10	200	$4,000.00	210	$4,200.00
10-Jun-16	SJ	00000020	Sale; Thomson	210	-80	($1,600.00)	130	$2,600.00
14-Jun-16	SJ	00000022	Sale; Tiffany Ca	130	-60	($1,200.00)	70	$1,400.00
17-Jun-16	SJ	00000023	Sale; Thomson	70	20	$400.00	90	$1,800.00
			Envelopes Larc		90	$1,800.00		
RR18			**Register Rolls**					
01-Jun-16	IJ	IJ000001	Inventory coun	0	10	$345.50	10	$345.49
04-Jun-16	PJ	00000018	Purchase; Davic	10	350	$12,090.91	360	$12,436.40
06-Jun-16	SJ	00000019	Sale; Horizon C	360	-60	($2,072.73)	300	$10,363.67
11-Jun-16	PJ	00000022	Purchase; Davic	300	-25	($863.64)	275	$9,500.03
13-Jun-16	SJ	00000021	Sale; Globe Tra	275	-70	($2,418.19)	205	$7,081.84
14-Jun-16	SJ	00000022	Sale; Tiffany Ca	205	-60	($2,072.73)	145	$5,009.11
21-Jun-16	SJ	00000025	Sale; Sally's Wa	145	-50	($1,727.28)	95	$3,281.83
27-Jun-16	SJ	00000028	Sale; Surf Store	95	-30	($1,036.37)	65	$2,245.46
			Register Rolls		65	$2,245.47		

Richmond Papars Pty Ltd
23 High Street
Richmond
VIC 3121

General Journal

01-Jun-16 To 30-Jun-16

ABN: 46 995 263 632

ID No.	Account No.	Account Name	Debit	Credit Job No.
GJ	**30-Jun-16**	**Depreciation**		
GJ000001	6-5100	Furniture Depreciation	$133.00	
GJ000001	1-2120	Accum. Depr. Furniture		$133.00
GJ000001	6-5200	Office Equipment Depreciation	$117.00	
GJ000001	1-2220	Accum. Depr. Office Equipment		$117.00
GJ000001	6-5300	Computer Depreciation	$83.00	
GJ000001	1-2320	Accum. Depr. Computers		$83.00
GJ000001	6-5400	Store Fittings Depreciation	$250.00	
GJ000001	1-2420	Accum. Depr. Store Fittings		$250.00
GJ	**30-Jun-16**	**Loan Instalment Breakdown**		
GJ000002	9-1000	Interest Expense	$114.36	
GJ000002	2-2100	Bank Loan	$185.64	
GJ000002	1-1110	Cheque Account		$300.00
		Grand Total:	$883.00	$883.00

* Year-End Adjustments
Page 1 of 1

Reconciliation Report

Richmond Papars Pty Ltd
23 High Street
Richmond
VIC 3121

ABN: 46 995 263 632

ID No.	Date	Memo/Payee	Deposit	Withdrawal

Account:	1-1110	**Cheque Account**		
Date Of Bank Statement:	30-Jun-16			
Last Reconciled:	30-Jun-16			
Last Reconciled Balance:	$59,822.64			

Reconciled Cheques

ID No.	Date	Memo/Payee	Deposit	Withdrawal
28	01-Jun-16	Richmond Real Estate		$1,100.00
29	07-Jun-16	Melbourne Insurance		$220.00
30	09-Jun-16	Gary Corporation		$9,375.00
31	16-Jun-16	Smith & Baker		$4,000.00
32	20-Jun-16	Victoria Electricity		$194.40
33	21-Jun-16	Australia Telecom		$215.84
34	24-Jun-16	Ian & Co. Pty Ltd		$4,000.00
SC300616	30-Jun-16	Bank Charges		$18.00
GJ000002	30-Jun-16	Loan Instalment Breakdown		$300.00
		Total:	$0.00	$19,423.24

Reconciled Deposits

ID No.	Date	Memo/Payee	Deposit	Withdrawal
CR0011	03-Jun-16	Payment; Peter Electronics	$10,000.00	
CR0012	06-Jun-16	Payment; Surf Stores	$8,400.00	
CR0013	10-Jun-16	Payment; Sally's Warehouse	$8,350.00	
CR0014	13-Jun-16	Payment; Western Estate Agents	$4,500.00	
CR0015	13-Jun-16	Payment; Horizon Designs	$5,235.00	
CR0016	18-Jun-16	Payment; Thomson Clothings	$3,000.00	
CR0017	20-Jun-16	Payment; Globe Travels Pty Ltd	$7,880.00	
CR0018	25-Jun-16	Payment; Tiffany Cakes	$6,090.00	
CR0019	27-Jun-16	Payment; Peter Electronics	$2,300.00	
		Total:	$55,755.00	$0.00

Outstanding Cheques

ID No.	Date	Memo/Payee	Deposit	Withdrawal
35	25-Jun-16	Melbourne Removals		$55.00
36	28-Jun-16	Mark & Tony		$4,900.00
37	28-Jun-16	Gary Corporation		$1,000.00
38	28-Jun-16	Smith & Baker		$1,840.00
		Total:	$0.00	$7,795.00

Reconciliation:		
AccountRight Balance On 30-Jun-16:	$52,027.64
Add: Outstanding Cheques:	$7,795.00
SubTotal:	$59,822.64
Deduct: Outstanding Deposits:	$0.00
Expected Balance On Statement:	$59,822.64

Page 1 of 1

Profit & Loss Statement

June 2016

Richmond Papars Pty Ltd
23 High Street
Richmond
VIC 3121

ABN: 46 995 263 632

Income		
Sales - A3 Copy Paper	$4,363.64	
Sales - A4 Copy Paper	$5,559.10	
Sales - A5 Copy Paper	$2,163.64	
Sales - Coloured Paper	$3,454.54	
Sales - Envelopes	$3,818.19	
Sales - Register Rolls	$13,254.54	
Total Income		$32,613.65
Cost Of Sales		
Cost Of Sales	$21,090.80	
Total Cost Of Sales		$21,090.80
Gross Profit		$11,522.85
Expenses		
General Expenses		
Bank Fees	$18.00	
Electricity Expenses	$176.73	
Telephone Expenses	$196.22	
Waste Removal	$50.00	
Total General Expenses		$440.95
Depreciation Expenses		
Furniture Depreciation	$133.00	
Office Equipment Depreciation	$117.00	
Computer Depreciation	$83.00	
Store Fittings Depreciation	$250.00	
Total Depreciation Expenses		$583.00
Insurance Expenses		
Business Insurance	$200.00	
Total Insurance Expenses		$200.00
Rent		
Rent	$1,000.00	
Total Expenses		$2,223.95
Operating Profit		$9,298.90
Total Other Income		$0.00
Other Expenses		
Interest Expense	$114.36	
Total Other Expenses		$114.36
Net Profit/(Loss)		$9,184.54

This report includes Year-End Adjustments.

Page 1 of 1

Richmond Papars Pty Ltd
23 High Street
Richmond
VIC 3121

Trial Balance

June 2016   ABN: 46 995 263 632

Account Name	Debit	Credit	YTD Debit	YTD Credit
Cheque Account	$28,536.76		$52,027.64	
Trade Debtors		$19,880.00	$11,370.00	
Inventory	$1,081.92		$9,909.45	
Furniture At Cost	$0.00		$8,000.00	
Accum. Depr. Furniture		$133.00		$399.00
Office Equipment At Cost	$0.00		$7,000.00	
Accum. Depr. Office Equipment		$117.00		$351.00
Computers At Cost	$0.00		$5,000.00	
Accum. Depr. Computers		$83.00		$249.00
Store Fittings At Cost	$0.00		$15,000.00	
Accum. Depr. Store Fittings		$250.00		$750.00
GST Collected		$3,261.35		$10,835.74
GST Paid	$2,379.57		$8,311.33	
Trade Creditors	$725.00			$21,550.00
Bank Loan	$185.64			$19,446.29
Owner's Capital		$0.00		$30,000.00
Sales - A3 Copy Paper		$4,363.64		$21,636.37
Sales - A4 Copy Paper		$5,559.10		$17,422.75
Sales - A5 Copy Paper		$2,163.64		$20,936.36
Sales - Coloured Paper		$3,454.54		$13,999.99
Sales - Envelopes		$3,818.19		$9,704.56
Sales - Register Rolls		$13,254.54		$25,036.35
Cost Of Sales	$21,090.80		$68,313.52	
Bank Fees	$18.00		$18.00	
Electricity Expenses	$176.73		$547.45	
Telephone Expenses	$196.22		$595.86	
Waste Removal	$50.00		$150.00	
Discounts Given	$0.00		$378.87	
Furniture Depreciation	$133.00		$399.00	
Office Equipment Depreciation	$117.00		$351.00	
Computer Depreciation	$83.00		$249.00	
Store Fittings Depreciation	$250.00		$750.00	
Business Insurance	$200.00		$600.00	
Rent	$1,000.00		$3,000.00	
Interest Expense	$114.36		$346.29	
Total:	$56,338.00	$56,338.00	$192,317.41	$192,317.41

This report includes Year-End Adjustments.

Page 1 of 1

Richmond Papars Pty Ltd
23 High Street
Richmond
VIC 3121

Balance Sheet

As of June 2016

ABN: 46 995 263 632

Assets		
Current Assets		
Bank Accounts		
Cheque Account	$52,027.64	
Total Bank Accounts		$52,027.64
Other Current Assets		
Trade Debtors	$11,370.00	
Inventory	$9,909.45	
Total Other Current Assets		$21,279.45
Total Current Assets		$73,307.09
Non-Current Assets		
Furniture		
Furniture At Cost	$8,000.00	
Accum. Depr. Furniture	($399.00)	
Total Furniture		$7,601.00
Office Equipment		
Office Equipment At Cost	$7,000.00	
Accum. Depr. Office Equipment	($351.00)	
Total Office Equipment		$6,649.00
Computers		
Computers At Cost	$5,000.00	
Accum. Depr. Computers	($249.00)	
Total Computers		$4,751.00
Store Fittings		
Store Fittings At Cost	$15,000.00	
Accum. Depr. Store Fittings	($750.00)	
Total Store Fittings		$14,250.00
Total Non-Current Assets		$33,251.00
Total Assets		$106,558.09
Liabilities		
Current Liabilities		
GST Liabilities		
GST Collected	$10,835.74	
GST Paid	($8,311.33)	
Total GST Liabilities		$2,524.41
Other Current Liabilities		
Trade Creditors	$21,550.00	
Total Other Current Liabilities		$21,550.00
Total Current Liabilities		$24,074.41
Non-Current Liabilities		
Bank Loan	$19,446.29	
Total Non-Current Liabilities		$19,446.29
Total Liabilities		$43,520.70
Net Assets		$63,037.39
Equity		
Owner's Capital	$30,000.00	
Current Year Earnings	$33,037.39	
Total Equity		$63,037.39

This report includes Year-End Adjustments.

Page 1 of 1

www.ingramcontent.com/pod-product-compliance
Lightning Source LLC
Chambersburg PA
CBHW060513060326
40689CB00020B/4725